THE FORLORN SIDE OF LIFE

SAFIA ALI

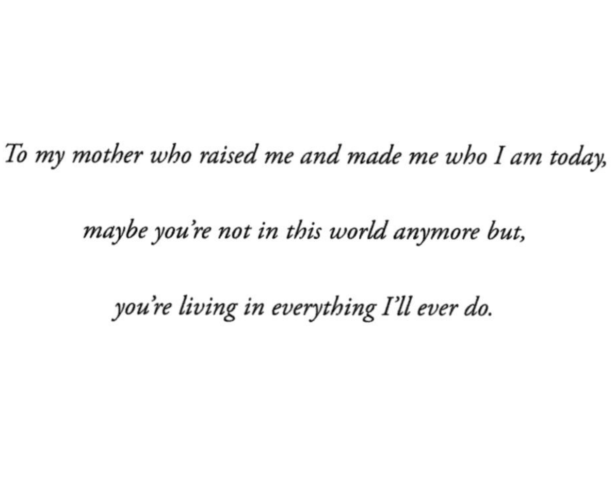

To my mother who raised me and made me who I am today,

maybe you're not in this world anymore but,

you're living in everything I'll ever do.

Contents

Contents

Contents

Contents

Foreword

As humans, what is the one thing we all share? Is it love? Organs? Dimensions? We all share oblivion.

The Forlorn Side Of Life is the most relatable, emotional collection I have ever come across. Poignant and triggering, the things it reflects...I never knew that words could be this powerful, this revolutionary.

Safia Ali beautifully weaves her way into grief and explaining it in the most delicate manner, takes us through the worst times of our lives in the best possible way. Awfully stunning, the book journeys us through getting, attaching, and then separating from things we love and reflects just how ugly and brutal and mean the universe can be.

Fearless, emotional and bold. I have never been more overwhelmed.

Preface

I have heard from people that life is nothing but a journey and we reach our destination after we die but if it is just a mere journey, why do we make connections that stay immortal and last for an eternity?

I have witnessed someone become an essential part of my life, she was not a person to me but she was my habit. I was used to being around her at all times and maybe that's why I never imagined losing her, I never thought I would have to live without her. She did everything for me, she became my mother, father and my dearest friend. I was never the one with a lot of close friends because in every friend, I tried to find parts of her but never really found it. Whenever I got sad over the fact that she is not here anymore, people would say, "She would want you to be happy" but out of the million things that she taught me, she forgot to teach me how to be happy without her. Now, *I hear words that make no sound but, with her I shared a silence that screamed so loud*, yet gave me the peace I still crave. For a long time after she was gone, I lived in denial constantly beacuse that was the first time I felt so many emotions at once. I was not ready to accept that I will never get to see her again and at some point I believed she would come back but obviously she cannot. I look for her in every person that claims to love me but no one can really love me like her. If only I could see her face once more and lie down next to her, it would be enough for the rest of my days.

"The Forlorn Side Of Life" is a collection of emotions that we feel when we lose someone closest to our heart. The feeling of grief,

loss, abandonment and homelessness is all we know at that moment. A million things wander around our mind but not even one of them is understandable. We cry for the life they didn't live and for the one they did. The regret of not acknowledging their efforts enough stays for a long time. Grief is a life-long emotion that never really goes away or fades with time, we learn how to live and continue with our life but there is always a void that is left behind and nothing or no one can fill that. They are everywhere but nowhere. They are in the silent whispers of the leaves, they are in the scent of rain and all the colours of rainbows. Grief does not make you weak, it is a sign of bravery. It shows that you are capable enough to feel that gut-wrenching pain everyday for the rest of your life.

All I really want in this life is to live a life worth watching because I know she is up there, watching over me. I wish to make her proud, I wish to be the person she wanted me to be.

Acknowledgements

My first debt is to my Godmother, my guide, my best friend and the one I miss the most everyday but specially through this journey, she made me who I am and I will be forever grateful to her. I would like to thank my parents who support me in everything I've ever done and I plan to do. A special thanks to myself because writing this book was a very personal journey full of fears, lack of confidence and self doubt but I went through it all because that was the right thing to do and a big hug and gratitude to Ashwera Hasan for the help she provided. I am incredibly thankful to my readers who appreciate my work and I hope this one will be a delight for you as well. Lastly, I would like to thank all those people who made me smile and cry even once because without you, I wouldn't learn to channel my emotions through poetry.

island view (i love you) <3.

Thank You All!

1. Long Lost Happiness.

The day that I lost you,
I lived my lavender-scented childhood,
in the last few moments we shared.
The memories where you held me,
closer than your heart,
the heart that still beats somewhere inside me.
I'm nothing more than a flower waiting to decease,
withering down every passing minute,
where I die a little everyday.
I lay down on your side of the bed with my eyes shut,
reminding the angels to take care of my angel.
I wait for you to sing me a lullaby,
make me feel something,
even for a span of seconds,
but you're nowhere to be found except my heart.
I can't see you or hold you,
I can't lay my head on your lap like I used to.
Yet you're still the only place that gives me peace,
the only person that reminds me of happiness.

2. The Destination.

One last time before she closed her eyes,
would you have liked to feel the warmth of her gaze?
"Just hug me goodbye one more time",
would you have said that before her soul fled away?
I hear the whispers of sweet nothings saying,
"I can understand, but you have to move on",
but somehow these (sweet) nothings fill poison,
in my veins and make me sob and wail.
At last,
When I'm nothing but the dust on the sidewalk,
I will still remember that sunlit face on a cloudy day,
those eyes that almost felt like the moon was glaring at me.
At that moment,
I will know that the destination of an angel,
will always be the heavens above.

3. Are You There?

A veil of illusion covers my sight,
the moment I felt your hand slip out of mine,
since that day my conscience died
and I've been burying parts of me alive.

I leave my sovereignty behind,
and maybe there's still a place holding,
stolen letters of you and I,
long lost and forgotten but always in my mind.

Your memories hit me like an ocean wave
but I never once fought back,
it would be similar to throwing punches in the air,
they all cheat but I've been fair.

When I hear your name,
it triggers a connection,
a syrup crystallised in amber,
all that is left is an illusion.

4. Nomadic Love.

It's a dangerous thing to do,
to make homes out of people.
The unsinkable ships sink too,
and all that was there,
is consumed by the oceans.
I'm still here,
in the middle of the street,
homeless and abandoned,
Nowhere to call home,
No one to be close to.
The pain strikes on my tongue
and the words shiver and die.
The darkness seems brighter than the light,
there's sun above my head,
but all I see is dusk at all times.
I pause, I stop and I freeze there,
in the middle of the street,
homeless and abandoned.

5. Two People, One Life.

I fidget around like a ghost,
in the hallways where we once stood
and I swore to always love you the most
maybe the universe misunderstood.

Listen to the ringing sound,
of my broken heart,
now that it's beating so loud,
ever since fate pulled us apart.

Every ounce of breath is a burden,
because there is nothing that can replace you,
but one thing is certain,
everything I'll ever do,
will always be about you.

6. Puzzle.

I know how it feels,
to have a heart that barely beats.
A life where it's all scattered around,
a godforsaken mess in it's own,
and the missing pieces are yet to be found.

I know how it feels,
to be alone in the crowd.
Where they offer you a bouquet of flowers,
only to block your lungs
so you can't breathe any longer.

I know how feels,
to lose the reason behind your existence,
yet continue existing,
without the one who taught you how to live,
and how to be.

And whenever my last day arrives,
only her name would be the one on my tongue.

She taught me a million things
but never once taught me,
how to live without her by my side.

7. My Heart is a Vault.

Never had it in me,
to release my grip
and let you slip,
my fingers would bleed for days.

Your fingers don't fit in mine anymore,
my hands feel empty without yours in it
but my heart feels heavier than the skies above
and it still bleeds where you reside.

Monsters and demons argue in my head,
whether I should stay in delusion
or let them haunt the corner,
that has known nothing but peace.

Guilt devours me inside out,
in every moment where we don't share a smile,
I try to let go of my angel
but we cannot be apart, you're locked in my heart.

8. Cold Abandonment.

The freezing cold outside is amusing to most people
whereas, I despise winters beyond anything.
Winters reek of chaos moving down the skin to the bones,
slowly and coldly poisoning each corner.

The child in me longs for a summer warmth,
where I could burn and melt, yet be safe.
Summer nights smell like my godmother's arms,
slowly caressing and putting me to sleep.

I'm aware, it's all me,
she's gone,
the summer nights still pass by,
but they are nothing similar,
they feel empty and meaningless.

9. She Completes Me.

Your heart beating in place of mine,
your happiness makes me smile,
you <u>live</u> in me,
in those corners,
where I only <u>existed</u> all this while.
Your soul knotted in mine,
the only place that comforts me,
is wherever you exist,
where I can hear you whisper,
where I can know that there is someone,
who reminds me of myself,
more than me.

10. Immortal Connection.

I often try to find love in places unknown to me,
somewhere away from my reach.
A place that is unfamiliar to my heart.

The only love I had known for most of my life,
is now gone and buried far beneath the ground.
I can't reach to the depths of that grave.

The deep lengths of the ground,
often remind me of how deep our love was.
Where my dreams collided with yours.

A place I've known longer than I remember,
that place is abandoned, that love is absent
but it still lives, where, you ask?

Deep inside me, my heart and my soul.
Forever and beyond.

11. Clandestine.

The secrets I hold so tight,
often slip away into tears,
when I'm thinking of all the ways,
you could be here
or
I could be there.
Just so I didn't have to perish alone,
in my mind where my demons are alive.
It's been years,
since you left.
I still can't say your name
or
talk about how you would lift me up,
on my lowest days,
only to leave me down here,
for evermore.

12. A Blank Notebook.

The blank pages compel me often,
to inscribe your name as soon as I hold the pen,
but I stifle,
I restrain,
because your name leads me to a place,
that's known to me yet so unfamiliar.
Where I resplendently stand so tall,
and the people who despise me,
they are nowhere around.
I feel a bedraggled home growing in my lungs,
a place where we are a family,
a place where we are unified,
but that place chokes to kill me when I cry,
it shoots to kill me when I try,
to leave and never come back.
But I'm compelled still,
to come back to you.
This home isn't a square, or a line or parallels,
that stay away from one another,
this home is a sphere and I return back,
again and again.

13. What Decides My Worth?

My body flecked with scars,
blood dripping off my nose
as I take off the mask.
I've lived in the corners,
and no one cared who I was,
until I put on a mask,
pretending to be someone I'm not,
distinct than my monsters,
who follow the pain and find me,
at the dead end of it all.
I burnt it, I burnt it all,
until there wasn't a shred of my past left
but somewhere inside,
I burnt parts of myself too and today,
when all of it has begun to end,
I find peace in watching them carry away,
the casket that holds parts of me,
that I murdered.

14. Celestial Skies.

I stay awake until the darkest hours,
because no matter how hard I pretend,
to be a realist,
I'm a dreamer after all.
I'm afraid that if I sleep,
I might dream of something,
something that is out of my reach,
or maybe something that is the closest to me
but can never be close to me.
I stay awake in the light of the moon,
and I tell the stars about my godmother.
The way her laugh sent glitters down my spine,
the way her glance made my heart smile .
When the stars hear about her,
they often abandon the constellations
and adore her amusing self,
and become fond of her,
just like I am.

15. Medicine.

You sat alone in the icy cold
but I would sit with you even if it froze me.
Your smile cured my brittle heart,
hence, you never shared your tears with me.
You stood alone in the cloudburst
but I would sit with you even if it drenched me.
I would give you my happiness,
I would give you my sunshine
but I assumed you had your own.
You have been the prey to yourself,
while I'd kill anyone who could hurt you.
You would never let me know,
that you're slowly fading in time.
Your touch healed me
but what if I get bruised,
would you leave the heavens and come back?

16. Remembrance.

The memories of you and I,
are hidden somewhere safe,
in the form of dusty photographs,
or a necklace hanging from my neck.

The love we shared,
is deep inside a corner of my heart,
where there's nothing but a void since you left,
and that is where you beat in the form of love.

I want you to be my protector,
I want to hide in your shelter,
a place where I feel at home,
a place where only you can find me.

17. There's Always Light.

I've been buried so deep beneath the ground,
away from light, right beside darkness
and there is no way I could go further down,
because this is the end of the earth above.
The only hope is that,
above every grave,
there's light and there's land,
where people reside,
and not the monsters.
I freeze in the cold,
insects devour on my flesh,
I wasn't of use as a person to any
now that I'm dead,
my flesh is food to many.
I wake up from the dreadful nightmare,
I tell myself that there's still light ahead,
I remind myself of the years that are to come,
I promise myself a life better than this.

18. Reverie.

I never knew what peace felt like,
until that one moment,
the most peaceful one in the chaos.
I submerged into the waters,
it covered the nooks and crannies of my existence,
while my hair danced with the flowing current.
That is when I felt like,
I am the owner of myself.
Constantly gasping and running out of breath,
but at the same time filled with all the oxygen.
I collect my scattered thoughts,
and fill them in a jar of solitude.
Sunlight gleamed like burning embers,
along the treetops twisted into melted shadows.
It clogged my ears with silence that is angry,
cursing me and shouting.
I drift alone for the rest of my life,
in my secret underwater chamber.

19. Ingenuity.

When reality exhausts your mind,
turn your head towards imagination,
That book, one of a kind,
all pages reeking of fascination.

These places I often visit,
keep me hooked and leave me wanting more,
my mind keeps fidgeting around the what-ifs,
and it cannot stay unlooked.

By the sheer volume of content,
I got swamped in that world,
what stays with me is the scent,
of all the parts, comes the one that swirled.

The characters start off,
as implausible caricatures ridiculously named,
I keep looking and cannot stop
but the irony arrives where the wilderness is tamed.

I feel as if it really exists somehwere in my mind,
and goes on and on for evermore.
When I try to leave, it holds me tighter and tighter,
and frustatingly I stay, but deep down that's what I wanted.

20. Destruction.

From the street, it looks like nothing
but invites me to shake the settled dust.
In the garden hung a weary old swing,
looking like it's waiting for the child in me.

Around there was a brickwork perfectly beneath the dust,
of years and rising upwards to the sky and clouds,
the ones that gave me an alarming, disturbing alert.
No doubt why it was so far away from the crowds.

My footsteps echoed on the wooden floor,
which scared and pleased me at once,
I slowly move away but it calls me closer and closer,
freezing, burning, I try to get away.

The door hinges squeak when opened,
and the windows are all shattered,
like my dreams, my heart and soul,
My house was after all,
<u>YOU.</u>

but it is destructed now.

21. Caliginosity.

Its's all blur in front of my eyes,
I can't see if you're close or far away.
My heart can't beat no matter how hard it tries,
I feel like I miss you now, more than ever.

My eyes long to see you but you're like the sun above my head,
if I look straight at you, I might lose sight of everything else
but your memories follow me no matter how hard I run,
it's all dark and there is no light as far as I can see.

Your voice is my most favourite song,
but now all I have is the radio's static noise.
I desire to have you, knowing that youre far gone,
and here, without you, is not where I belong

22. Transient.

I had a dream last night,
and I woke up full of fright.
The dream was not scary
but it was more than happy,
I fear happiness,
because it never lasts,
neither did the dream,
nor did you.

23. Ally.

Chaos is not evil, it never was.
Chaos is a baby crying out of hunger.
Chaos is a person playing with their puppy,
and chaos is the loud grief coming out of my heart.
Chaos can be anything but evil,
there is a beautiful innocence in all the chaos,
everything that is loud is not unpleasant to the ears.
Chaos is soothing and loving.

Peace was never a friend of mine,
but chaos never left me.

24. Twilight.

If you look deep into darkness,
it's not your nemises.
You can pull the curtains,
and invite the darkness.
Hear it from a night owl's perspective,
it will tell you that darkness makes it feel alive,
even more than the brightest of days.
Darkness is the epitome of loyalty,
even after the loathe it recieves,
comes back everyday.
If I wasn't in the dark,
bright mornings would be,
nothing special to me

25. Ruination.

It was all a matter of seconds,
she took her last breath,
life left her hand,
and death held her close.

I used to believe death comes with age,
but we don't understand,
dying is certain
but the timing is not.

The dark shadow of death,
is always somewhere around,
the universe gave us life
and it can take it away too.

26. Childhood Home.

I spell my name in broken letters,
as I walk towards the town,
that has been left alone.
The fragrance of the flowers,
has departed long ago.
The mango and guava trees,
don't bear the delicious fruits anymore.
All the grass has grown taller and wilder,
and I feel small in front of it.
Maybe the summer days,
that I kept reminiscing about,
has come back to me,
when I used to run around the gardens,
when the grass was short and tamed,
and the trees still had fruits hanging down,
the flowers still contained the sweet smell.
This home,
this time
is a different place.

27. Long Forsaken.

I'm an empty house,
waiting for someone,
to make it home.
I stand old and rusted,
with footprints of mud,
on my floor,
I just want someone,
to tidy me up,
free of dust and spider-webs.
I just want someone,
to fill the empty porcelain vase,
with a posy of primroses.
I'm an empty house,
waiting for someone,
to make it home,
and come to me,
when they feel alone.

28. Forbearance.

My heart was burning,
and I kept wondering,
will there be an end,
to all my suffering?
I offered others roses,
but I silently walked on thorns.
Only because,
their loss would not be my win.
Only because,
what had been written for me,
was written by the greatest of writers.

29. Untold Words.

I looked over my shoulder to see what's behind,
I saw a land so unknowingly familiar.
I remember the smell of the rain,
that suddenly started to smell like poison.
Where I lived, wasn't a home,
it was just a house.
Home is the place,
where I belong.
Home is where they wait for you,
and they waited for me for ages.
I left them like a grave so forgotten,
but my soul promised to return,
home.
The graves looked like grass,
grown so lushly on the earth.
The graveyard is my garden tonight.
My bones twisted,
and fire melted it all,
everything dripped down,
like tears that I've held for so long.

30. Blame Game.

If tomorrow starts without me,
and your temptations seem to overwhelm you,
while you're busy reminiscing about me
but I'm far away and gone.

Would you be curious to know why I left?
I was always proven wrong as long as I was here,
hence, I decided to leave,
because my existence bothered each one of you.

I hope you know, I wasn't so bad,
but the devil around everyone could never get that.
I felt small and misunderstood,
but how does it matter, anyway?

All of them wanted me gone,
I fulfilled all the wishes they held.
Now, they are busy reminiscing about me,
while I'm far away and long gone.

31. A Trap.

I often find myself wandering far away,
where memories of the past stay.
You ask me how I am,
I don't answer that,
instead, I tell you about a traumatic phase.

You ask me about my family,
but I tell you things I reminisce.
I want nothing but to forget all that,
it makes me feel weak and I hate that.

I wanna get out of this,
a whole lifetime I've been stuck,
in this mind of mine.

32. Dream.

I still feel,
the texture of her hair,
on the tip of my fingers,
when I dream about her.
The brown hair,
coaxed into tiny ringlets,
and my fingers,
running through them.
A dream that was true once,
but only hurts me everyday now.

33. Yearning.

I suddenly look down,
found myself dressed in all white.
Pure white cloth,
stained with blood all around.

I stopped and looked back,
all I saw was a deathbed behind me,
and someone from the above calling me
Is it time yet?

I felt my knees breaking down,
as I fall on the ground,
the moon screamed blood all around
and the stars disappeared.

I felt a power,
taking something out of me,
it was nothing else
but my soul leaving my body.

I still wish all these things came true,
I wish it was me instead of you.
I wish the creator calls me,
or the destroyer chases me.

34. Unfeasible.

I can't comprehend,
whether the darkness inside me is darker,
or the one outside where I stand.
They say it's known as,
the graveyard of feelings where the immortal souls reside,
they understand nothing but the language of,
bloodtears and agony.
The mellifluous melody,
that once poured sleep in my ears,
now sound like,
the scariest screaming which depicts fears.
I still keep wandering here in the middle of nowhere,
driving myself into nothingness,
waiting to bid an impossible farewell.

35. I Know Better.

At nights,
when sleep doesn't reside in my eyes,
I wonder how it would be,
if those days came back.
When you were with me,
all the time.
If I didn't know better,
I'd believe that you're still around.
Do you still listen when I talk to you?
and shed those golden words at me.
Your smile still wakes me,
and I can't wake up anymore.
Your belongings don't belong to me,
they didn't leave none for me.
Do you still sing your favourite songs for me?
trying to put me to sleep,
holding me like a baby
and loving me forever.

36. Don't Let Go.

No matter ho many places I looked into,
I never walk past your shadow anymore,
everyone is moving forward,
but I refuse to move a foot.
I want to stay there forever,
where you and me,
were together.
I'll never be sad,
I'll never shed tears,
but I'll never move ahead,
from your memories,
and your little jokes,
and I request you too,
to never let go.

37. Oath.

If it's written amidst the stars,
that are souls will collide,
then maybe,
just maybe,
even the stars lie sometimes.
Slowly one day,
dreaming of your cosmos,
I will sleep through the time,
and maybe in the next life,
you will be next to me.

38. Comfort.

I can't let go of you,
because there is comfort,
in what has already passed.
It kills me,
breaks me,
and yet I can't step out.
I can't stop loving you,
knowing that I'll never,
have you back.
You're the place that brings me peace,
and the place that gives me a reason.

39. Take Over Me.

I know I will eventually have to let go,
of the places I came from,
to move to places that take me forward.
To let go of homes,
because homes break in no time,
and leave you longing for something,
that wasn't even yours.

40. Hiding Spot.

I'll make sure nobody knows,
that I'm still in some unknown corner,
of your heart.
This is where I reside,
because I have nowhere to go.
I'll be homeless,
if you throw me out,
I have no way back,
and no way forward.
My home is your heart,
every other place,
cuts me down and breaks me down.

41. Fantasy.

The love,
the fright,
the happiness,
and the fight,
to lose you drives me mad.
You are all I know,
I break down and slip,
through the cracks,
of your memories.
A nightmare is stuck,
in my mind,
the shadows that scare me,
the one tale I can't escape,
there one where I'm with you,
and you are with me too,
but only in my head.

42. Deafening.

Chaos is a part of me,
but I speak nothing better than silence,
I never knew silence could be,
so deafening,
it rings through my ears to reach my soine,
making it's way to
kill me and throw me.

43. Treasure.

I will continue to find your chaos,
in the silence of the night sky,
where there is nothing but,
my will to lose myself,
just so I can find you.
I am a barren land,
where nothing grows,
except all of your love.

44. Consumption.

I say nothing but tonight,
before I sing ballads to this season,
before my name is nothing more,
than a tide whispering mystery,
before I make a home,
among the long lost stars,
I will remind these spaces,
that your love is what kept me alive.
The uncountable times,
when I heard your voice,
set my heart aflame and free.

45. Would You Recognise Me?

I can't help but wonder,
if you ever see me again,
when time acts on me,
would you recognise me by my smile?
and tell me that it still looks the same.
If I look at you,
the same way I used to,
would you recognise me by my glare?
and tell me that my eyes haven't changed a bit.
I don't know,
how long will it take,
before I see you again,
but however long it takes,
I know I'm destined to end,
with my head on your lap.

46. Not For Me.

Last night,
I dreamt of a place,
where the stars would walk you home,
to me,
and I wouldn't be alone,
unaware of how your touch feels.
i dreamt of a morning,
where you will be the sunshine,
to me,
and I wouldn't stand alone in the dark,
unaware of how much light you have inside.
I dreamt of a lot of things,
where you would be beside me,
but everything is not for everyone.

47. Again and Again.

As unusual as it sounds,
I can be the sun that drowns every night,
just to let you, breathe as the moon.
I'll share my light with you,
when you suffer through,
the darkness of your own.
It's ironic how I never sleep,
but I always find myself dreaming,
of everything we could have had.
It feels so real,
but I come back to my senses,
and feel the life,
being sucked out of me.
You slowly drift away,
and fade into oblivion again,
I feel empty without you,
again.

48. If I was...

If I was a bird,
blue and feathery,
you would be my sky,
the only place where,
I feel free.
If I was a tiny grain of sand,
residing by the waters,
you would be my ocean,
the only thing,
that touches my soul.
If I was a person,
loved by none,
numb and inconsistent,
worried and stressed,
you would be my home,
the only place that owns me,
the only place that brings me peace,
the only place,
that will truly ever know me.

49. The Sea.

You are like the sea,
your love consumes me,
it comes crashing down,
like waves to the shore of my heart.
I have always been loved half,
but your love hides me in it,
and covers my ears from,
all the curses they spill.
The waves have stopped,
they stay where my heart is,
right where they belong.

50. Last Few Seconds.

Look at me with those beautiful eyes,
hold me in those warm arms,
kiss me on my forehead because,
this day will not come back.
Rest your head on my shoulder,
while I sing you a lullaby.
Hold my hand through every second,
while I let the demons follow behind.
I'll give you a good night hug,
and you will have a peaceful sleep,
unaware and heedless.
I'll cry sitting next to you,
before I let you slip away,
before I let you go forever.
A wish that I often let out,
to call your name,
in my last days,
just like you did.

51. Nothingness.

I don't exist in this body anymore.
My existence lies in the restless sea,
waiting to drown me in it,
waiting to love me whole.
My soul resides in the moon,
full of craters,
the flaws,
the beauty,
altogether.
I am the end,
I'm free and alone.
i wander in the depths of the earth,
and I wonder,
If I had someone,
who looked at me,
like poetry lies inside of me.
I feel incapable of their love,
because there exists a massive garden inside me,
that knows nothing but everything,
that is not meant for me.
I look at you,
and I drift myself,
into nothing and nothingness.

52. Would You?

They are too blind to see,
the stars I hold in my fist,
waiting to decorate their eyes.
They are too blind to see,
how I think of them every second,
before anyone else but,
what if my heart stopped beating?
Would you still reside in me if I was lifeless?
If my heart freezes of cold,
and it can't be compassionate anymore.
Would you give me warmth?
If my ashes rose up to life,
would you live in me again?
If I give up the oxygen,
would you stop breathing too?

53. I'm The Monster.

When I look in the mirror,
pieces of glass jab in my eyes.
When I look at the person,
standing in the mirror,
it reminds me of a poison that kills.
"No! that's not true, you saved lives."
says an inner voice,
"But you killed so many too."
says the other.
Maybe I'm the cure,
a life saver,
or maybe I'm a curse,
that makes them suffer,
doesn't kill but makes them wish,
to get rid of me.
Maybe I'm a toxin,
the one they gulped down
but now it doesn't come out,
neither can be swallowed whole.
I'm a killer,
I'm the trigger to your gun,
or maybe I'm the gun myself.
Using someone else's shoulder,

to kill and murder.
Like resurrecting the dead,
bring out the cure,
and let go of death.

54. All of Me is All of You.

Sometimes I wish,
I stopped writing about you.
My words reek of pain and agony,
they are just wasted air,
from a withering lung,
and no one is paying attention.
Sometimes I wish,
I forgot about you,
but my life wouldn't mean anything if I did,
everything I do would be for nothing,
because when I reach,
into the deep corners of my heart,
there is a lot,
you have left in me.

55. My Life.

They are so far above feeling anything,
so far away from being human,
living a life that starts as a race,
and end with death.
My life is like a river,
flowing to it's mother ocean.
Learning through the way,
crashing through the mountains,
bumping into rocks,
seeing all of,
day and night,
summer and winter,
and finally reaching home,
to its mother,
just like I will,
someday.

56. Proximity.

I guess,
I'll love you,
the way the sun,
loves the moon,
and you will love me,
the way the grass,
loves the trees,
always together,
but never really close.

57. Query.

In a piece of you,
I lost my whole being,
you're where I live,
you're where I reside.
I pluck my soul,
into small pieces,
to make you a perfume,
so you'll think of mr,
once through the day.
Out of every word,
that comes out of my mouth,
I promise the ones I speak to you,
will always be true.
After all I do,
will you remember to forget me?

58. Above.

I'm a voice unheard,
I'm a letter forgotten.
What am I here for?
when each one of you hate me.
The one who adored me,
the one who is long gone,
made me feel like a poem,
meaningful and beautiful.
Now, I feel like,
my name is not a name,
but a word with no true meaning.
The skies above,
look like a perfect place to fly,
happily and freely.

59. List of Almost(s).

I often hide,
in the shadows that never left me,
it feels like a threshold,
one that I'm not allowed to cross.
I stood in the rain,
deserted,
abandoned,
only to wait for someone,
who was way ahead,
of the paths that could lead,
her to me
or
me to her.
I was yearning,
for us to be together,
for us to be a soul,
in different bodies,
but my soul has been demolished,
and your soul has departed.
Your soul holds a map of memories,
I'll keep visiting,
as long as I live,
a house that can never be mine,

a residence that rejects my existence.

I have a list of almosts,

that I couldn't touch.

I have words,

lodged in my throat,

succumbing on my lips,

to be heard by you.

60. A Bubble That Bursts.

I have bumped into,
a lot of people.
I have written poems,
about several.
I have lived for a few years,
but none of them,
was as wonderful,
as the ones where,
I had you,
next to me.
Love touched me,
but didn't stay.
You promised me,
but didn't stay.

61. Strangers.

I'm waiting for you,
to break the silence,
just like I broke myself,
in a million ways to find you.
In search of you,
I lost pieces that I had,
I lost everything,
that brought us close.
Are you a stranger to me now?

62. Moon.

You disappeared,
but I feel your presence,
and your touch,
as I stand under the sun.
It feels as bright and cheerful as you,
and I'm standing here,
looking for you.
You left a bunch of memories,
that I'll hold onto,
just like you held me in your arms.
I could be nonexistent,
but I can't,
because the only reason,
why I'm existing without you,
is because I'm looking for you,
in every person,
and every place.
At night,
I sit and talk to the moon,
what if you're talking to me too.

63. Blank Canvas.

I was born a blank canvas,
but you filled me with colours.
The blues became my scars,
the red circles defined my past,
the purple parallel lines disguised as our story
and the pink squares depicted my despair.
I wonder why,
you're no longer the truth I fought for,
and you're not even the answer to my how(s).
I thought I had nothing to lose,
until I lost the most precious gem.
I'm stil waiting at God's back door,
waiting for you to open the door,
and tell me that you will stay this time.
These caressing words sound like broken letters,
but they don't matter anymore.
I'm here rotting an waiting,
constantly and continously.

64. Delusive.

I asked them to shed light on,
why I'm alive in their nightmares.
I broke all mirrors that surrounded me,
an ugly self cannot be disguised.

65. Reassurance.

The clouds stood still,
when I called your name,
to feel you,
to touch you,
because no matter,
how far we are,
the clouds reassure me,
that you're watching over me,
from the stars.

66. Death.

I died,
but my death wasn't the way,
it was supposed to be.
they didn't recognise,
and I was unknown to myself too.

My outcry today,
is to live once again,
only to see you,
because what's the point of death,
if I don't die for you.

I want to live again,
to touch you,
feel you,
see you.

Only to close my eyes,
once and forever,
I want to live,

once again,
only to die for you.

67. Nameless.

They block the memories,
that remind them of me.
They overshadow my existence,
like a piece of paper in trash.
I'm the one who has lunch alone,
the one who is cropped out of pictures,
and cut out of lives.
Today,
I am nameless.
I don't have a name,
they can curse anymore.
but I'm sure,
the things I write,
they are enough to,
recognise me by.

68. Ignition.

My love is weeping tonight,
under the tree, where we used to talk.
Those conversations are left incomplete,
but they'll continue to live inside me,
as long as my lungs fight to stay alive.

My emotions are sleeping tonight,
somewhere behind the purple colour so bright.
Those purple flowers are crushed beneath their feet,
they live in denial and kill their desires,
the don't fight for the things their soul ignites for.

The blood is creeping on my feet tonight,
right where I stand still,
where our love was killed.
It was killed and that's for sure,
but it will take birth stronger than before.

69. Fabrication.

In my restless nights,
I wait for you to come back home,
to sit beside me
and hold my hand.
When I can't find peace,
in anything around,
I wait for you to come back home,
to caress my hair
and put me to sleep.
I wait for you everyday,
I know you can't come back,
there is no way you could,
but if you do,
promise to love me more and more everyday,
and make up for the days,
when I couldn't feel your love.

70. Fire.

I don't know what to say,
but I'm here in front of you,
to tell you
that you have hurt me too.
Unintentionally,
leaving me behind,
with faces known,
but souls unfamiliar.
I was used to,
being in your protection,
but now I'm barefoot,
on a sunny day.
Now I'm drenched,
in the rain.
Now I'm burning,
in the desire,
to have you back.

71. Never Again.

This story, this hour, belongs to my mind,
when God pulls the curtains down,
and it's all dark.
I lay down on my bed,
with tears rolling down my cheek,
and I get tucked away,
into another memory,
fabricated with beautiful moments.
Sometimes, I open the door and wish,
that I'll see you standing in front of me.
Sometimes, when I cry, I wish,
you'd hold my hand and tell me it's okay.
These are just memories,
that make me smile,
and then cry,
then curse myself and feel the remorse.
I close my eyes,
and again,
it's all dark in front of me,
I lay down and take an oath,
to never wake up again.

72. I'm Resting.

I stood there, blankly, every night staring at that coffin,
because one day, that's where everyone will end up.
I saw a face destroyed with fire,
and melted with water.
I heard the voices inside me saying,
that I broke myself piece by piece.
The grave wasn't mine,
but it felt familiar,
I closed my eyes and.....shut.
The coffin's lid closed
and the hinges creeked,
a noise that deafens me,
to every other voice.
I wake up,
I sleep,
I walk
and I hide.
A living dead is what they call me,
but do I have another choice?
I saw my heart resting in the coffin's depth,
way before I heard them,
pronouncing me dead.
I'm resting,

I'm resting,
I'm resting,
but never in peace.

73. Hazy Image.

Your blur image is getting hazier in my eyes,
it feels like today,
I'm living that day again,
the day I saw you,
close your eyes forever
and in that moment,
a great mountain of remorse,
built up inside of me.
I saw you slowly fluttering your eyes,
and closing them.
I often reminiscence about,
your smile,
it had me struck,
every single time.
I thought we had a lifetime,
we didn't.

74. Lead Me to You.

The road less travelled by,
promises to take me to you,
where cobblestones look like,
pieces of destroyed graves
and the pavements smell like blood.
I follow the draped plants and scattered petals,
but I never reach you.
I mirror your behaviors and habits,
just to feel like I am you.
Your love glitters on my skin,
and my tears drop like pearls,
none of it will ever be enough.
Since the day you left,
I've been cutting myself down,
and I can't find a single part of me now.

75. No End.

They expected me to find somewhere,
but I woke up each night,
fidgeted around the hallway,
hoping that you'd pass by.
I'm lonely in the sense,
that not just anyone's company would suffice.
I kept staring at the pinned up pictures,
with mellifluous voices playing in my head.
I wish I had known better,
their withered ways were a way,
of telling me to move
but I'll stay forever and ever.
Nothing simply ends,
with a 7 letter word,
goodbye.

76. Waiting.

Under twenty feet of snow,
and twenty more to go,
that is where I still wait for you.
My hesitant hands will always,
find your fingertips to trace.
My colour coded emotions,
will always be connected with yours.
You're too far from where I am,
yet I still wait for you,
in every breath I take.

77. Fill The Spaces.

I sleep with one pillow under my head,
and one next to me,
because I need something,
to fill the empty space,
whether it's my bed or my heart.
My heart carries a void,
and no matter how many people,
I let into my heart,
they never really fit into it.
My careless words slip off,
and they leave,
like a loaded gun.

78. What Did You Leave?

The only thing that,
takes the burden off my heart,
are my words,
but the irony speaks for itself,
my words are everything,
that reminds me of you.
The enticing lagoon of desires,
is filled with my wishes to see you.
Our souls might try,
to reach one another
but mine doesn't even exist anymore.
The only thing you left behind,
is the idiotic fool that I am.

79. Millionth Time.

Burn this letter down to ashes,
once you're done reading it.
I learnt lessons,
I smiled,
I laughed,
and I cried,
but every second,
I hear my heart break,
like glass shatters on floor.
You left me no choice but to,
try and try,
and die,
a million little times.

80. Killing Spree.

The crescent moon pierces the sky,
the dagger pierces my heart.
I could feel you fading away,
but you went too fast.
I'm still in the room where you stayed,
I'm frozen and can't move,
I cause no harm but,
I'd kill to see you,
one more time.

81. End Of Summer.

The reality of nightmares,
is that it scatters bones,
amongst my sanity and madness,
and fills it with a lake of lies and cobwebs.
As autumn casts a veil over summer,
all I can feel is shame.
Silk ribbons of darkness,
tied around my neck,
pull it once and watch my end.

82. Night Everyday.

The vivacious fire spreads in the room,
but I can only see you.
Bottles brim with desires,
but I can only feel you.
Sirens blare around me,
but I can only hear you.
Your nightmares haunt my narrative,
the dawn blooms,
but my days only started with you.

83. Prison.

I wish I could spill lies on this paper,
where none of it would be true.
All my heartbreaks,
would be known as achievements,
and all my pain would be sore.
I wish I could melt in the rain,
and be gone forever,
without a trace left behind.
I wish I could stay quiet,
and never make a sound again,
because my words are my own prison,
and I won't ever be free.

84. Apology.

I carry parts of my past,
that I couldn't bury properly.
I hold them like an armour,
whenever someone attacks me.
I've stared at the sky,
and the ceiling for hours,
without blinking.
You taught me a secret language,
and I've been fluent in it,
with no one to speak to.

85. Good-Night.

You promised me,
you wouldn't sleep,
without saying good-night.
Now, it's 4 a.m.
and you're nowhere around.
The night feels heavy,
like I'm carrying,
the moon and all the stars on my back.
I cannot forget you,
and I couldn't sleep a second,
without your sugar-coated goodbye.
Every second,
my soul crumbles into pieces,
I loathe myself,
because I'm so weak,
told hold onto you,
I'd die if I didn't.

86. Recipe Of A Home.

The bricks and stones,
would build a home,
and it wouldn't even matter,
because I'll be stuck in it,
forever alone.

87. Burning Witches.

I'm going to be everyone's nightmare,
everyone who has ever hurt me,
everyone who has pulled me apart.
They twisted my soul into shadows,
and you stood there watching me perish.
You burned me into ashes,
hunted me like a witch and pried on me,
with everyone who despised me.
I will never be vengeful towards you,
because I am not you.

88. Feeling.

I forgave everyone but myself,
and things are getting bad again.
I feel every insult,
like a sharp dagger.
I feel my dreams rotting,
under my pillow-cover,
and I feel this way all the time.

89. I'll Leave.

I make the world shatter,
and shake on my fingertips,
but I couldn't make you stay.
This time,
I will leave,
I will disappear into thin air,
because if I abandoned,
everything and everyone,
no one cold ever abandon me,
again.

90. If I Am.

My grief was discreet,
hidden somewhere,
between the pages of my notebook.
You'd never know if I'm suffering,
or I'm on the highest cloud.
I put bandages on my invisible wounds,
and let the visible ones bleed.
If I'm tired of being a warrior,
would anyone fight for me?
If I'm tired of existing,
would anyone live for me?

The End...

And just like the numbers in my life,
the numbers in the book,
remain 90,
and never a complete 100.

<3

THANK YOU....

9 798886 065039

Printed by Libri Plureos GmbH in Hamburg,
Germany